How to
Simplify
and have
Freedom
in
your
Life

Six Steps to Live Healthy in Mind, Body and Spirit

HAE S. BOLDUC

BALBOA.PRESS
A DIVISION OF HAY HOUSE

Balboa Press books may be ordered through booksellers or by contacting:

Balboa Press
A Division of Hay House
1663 Liberty Drive
Bloomington, IN 47403
www.balboapress.com
1 (877) 407-4847

Because of the dynamic nature of the Internet, any web addresses or
links contained in this book may have changed since publication and
may no longer be valid. The views expressed in this work are solely those
of the author and do not necessarily reflect the views of the publisher,
and the publisher hereby disclaims any responsibility for them.

The author of this book does not dispense medical advice or prescribe the use
of any technique as a form of treatment for physical, emotional, or medical
problems without the advice of a physician, either directly or indirectly. The
intent of the author is only to offer information of a general nature to help
you in your quest for emotional and spiritual well-being. In the event you use
any of the information in this book for yourself, which is your constitutional
right, the author and the publisher assume no responsibility for your actions.

Any people depicted in stock imagery provided by Getty Images are
models, and such images are being used for illustrative purposes only.
Certain stock imagery © Getty Images.

Print information available on the last page.

ISBN: 978-1-9822-4110-0 (sc)
ISBN: 978-1-9822-4111-7 (e)

Balboa Press rev. date: 01/28/2020

Contents

Preface

In order to have health for life in mind, body and sprit, we must have balance in six areas - relationships, career, finances, body, environment, and spirit. There are many intelligent people in this universe. However, we must have more than intelligence; we must have common sense and wisdom to achieve balance in these areas to feel the resulting freedom. It's not difficult, and you don't have to be a rocket scientist to figure this out. You just need discipline, and tenaciously work toward making daily progress! Life brings many unexpected challenges along the way. Nevertheless, life also gives us joy when we give 110% and progress through those challenges. We are only here once. We must always try to do our best in order to leave a positive mark on this earth.

Everyone wants to be happy and healthy. The key is discipline and execution. You can't just dream about wants and needs. You must start executing the steps to get your wants and needs. If you want to be rich, you may keep trying to make more money. A better approach is to focus on living within your means and saving funds for a rainy day! You can make more money, but if you are spending more than you are bringing in, you will always have a deficit – it's that simple. The more material possessions you own, the more material possessions you have to maintain! What if you own less? Then you will have more time to enjoy life rather than wasting time on purchasing, maintaining, and organizing the many possessions.

Foreword

Live magically! That motto is part of Hae's email signature. When I see her email signature, I can't help but think that life is magical for me. I feel so fortunate being married to and having such a wonderful relationship with Hae. She is the most beautiful and amazing person I know. Believe me when I tell you that I have said this so many times, and in public, to so many people, that some are getting used to (or tired of) hearing it. Hae and I are living the dream, and it is about time Hae wrote this pocket guide to share the philosophy of a great life. Life should be about having fun. The components of a great life are laid out in this book. Just remember to give back and help others along the way. Life is magical. by Craig Hafer

Chapter 1

Relationships

. . . .

"When you stop expecting people to be perfect, you can like them for who they are." – Donald Miller

~relationships are like the wild
ocean, never a dull moment~

Loving Partner, Soul Mate

It's never 50/50. You get more when you give/do more for your lover, spouse, partner. You get back more than you ever expected. Try the following techniques to surprise yourself, to be happy, and to thrive.

A true partner is someone emotionally close to share the ups and downs and the in-betweens of life. It means having someone who puts you first before themself and expresses compassion, brings you a cup of hot tea when you're sick or feeling down, helps you care for aging parents, and supports you in every way. It means someone who will be your partner in adventure, fun, and play. It means having someone close who is 110% (or 111% in the case of my spouse) invested in your success, your passion, your health, and your happiness.

1. It's tenacious, exhausting, and fun work giving 110%. It's also continuous, not just one day or one time or one week; it's a lifetime of working together! It is accomplishing those goals together that are difficult and/or impossible to accomplish alone.

2. Set a weekly distraction-free time for a serious or not so serious conversation with your partner. No device or online distractions, and

no children or animals (dogs and cats are also excluded) distractions. Give 110% attention to your partner's words, facial gestures, and body language, and hear your hearts beating in synchronicity.

3. Have a date day once a week for a movie and/or dinner, to visit local attractions, to discover new walking/hiking trails, or to visit a nearby town or city - an entirely fun joint activity. Explore the possibilities, spread your wings, and let your hearts soar.

4. At the beginning of each calendar year develop a joint roadmap, and plot out your dreams and goals to support each other's life journeys, and to be on the same page knowing what you both want to accomplish for the year. The roadmap may include visiting family, vacationing, running a marathon, health and self care goals, home projects such as growing a garden, painting the house, remodeling the kitchen or bathroom - whatever you both want to accomplish.

5. Have at least one grand vacation per year for escape from the mundane daily activities, to

rejuvenate, to celebrate your anniversary and birthdays, and to simply recharge.

6. Be vulnerable and willing to open up with your partner and communicate whatever is on your mind. No one is perfect; be willing to share your past mistakes, triumphs, upbringing, and how you raised your kids if you are in your second or third marriage. Knowing what you know today, be willing to look back and feel remorse for the imperfect way you lived your life and for the poor choices you made. Hindsight is always 20/20, and learning from the past is wisdom.

7. Reminisce about the first date with your loved one and the creative ways for impressing him/her. Continue to be creative and innovative in ways to inspire variety in your relationship!

Healthy Family

I have yet to witness a "perfect" family. There are invariably some quirky things or person(s) in the family, always. My husband and I are both in our second marriage and between us we have five grown children from our first marriages. His children and mine were raised in different environments with different life values. The only way to bridge and maintain a healthy family relationship is to accept the children's choices, no matter their selection of careers, their spousal choices, their location of residence, their looks, or their political and religious preferences. Accept them without judgment. No one is more superior than anyone else. Everyone is unique and what matters the most is the individual's love and happiness. At the end of day the most important part of life is family!

1. Love them unconditionally – We always think we want something in return when we give material things, time, or even a thank you note. How about accepting your family for who they are and love them unconditionally? This can be very difficult to do, but when you reach your own state of peace and balance, loving them comes naturally. Love does not cost anything; it's free and abundant. You never run out of it. The more you give, the more you receive.

2. Learn to forgive and move on from any past judgments and mistakes; at least periodically attempt to open up communication. Shutting down communication as if everything is OK is not going to resolve issues that have been building

up internally for years. And not forgiving and not moving on is not healthy for two people and the environment between them. Be honest with yourself and tell the other person that you have made mistakes and ask for forgiveness for whatever you have or haven't done. Give them the opportunity to tell you about their issues; forgive each other and move forward.

3. Schedule a family reunion at least twice a year. At the end of life, your family is the most important. Your friends may move to other parts of the world and may have completely forgotten about you. Your family is always with you no matter where they live and their stage in life. Holidays may be a difficult time to get together because of higher seasonal costs and the busy stressful time of year. To minimize expenses, tensions, and scheduling conflicts, meet either before or after a holiday. Find a mutually enjoyable location for all family members and share the unconditional love for each other!

4. Schedule mother and daughter or father and son time. In 2016, I started mother and daughter time with both my mother and with my

daughter. I visited my 96 year old mom in South Korea, who was living by herself. During my visit I cleaned the house and did the shopping and cooking. I slept with my mom and chatted about my early childhood memories. This time with my mother was not only rewarding for me, but I felt great relief knowing that I had spent precious time with my mother. Also for the first time in many years, I visited and spent similar quality time with my daughter, sharing my early childhood memories and my memories of her early childhood. We talked of many things about which I had never previously opened up. For example, I told her how very difficult life was raising her and her brother with very limited means. One Christmas, the only thing we could afford and had under the Christmas tree was her one piece sleeping pajamas and one shirt for her brother. We received one piece of clothing each; that was it. But in the end, it does not matter how many toys and clothes you receive for Christmas. The kids grow up very strong, emotionally and physically, independent, and levelheaded. Tough times along with the many life lessons make us strong.

Before my first husband passed away, he and our son got together often. They adored each other so much. They taught each other practical life lessons and just had fun conversing about their ideas as if they were best friends. Time spent together with loved ones are the most precious and you should always seek more of those times. All of us are here for a very brief period of time, so don't waste it.

5. Celebrate family successes – "And never miss a party if you can help it" - Sam Berns

Be happy for your child's new job, their new baby, or any event that calls for a get together celebration; these occasions build deeper bonds. In February 2017, my son and his wife, my daughter and her husband, and my husband and I spent quality time together. We rented a lake house in Maine for a week of together time. My son and daughter-in-law surprised us all by announcing the upcoming addition to their family, our granddaughter. This was wonderful news and we all screamed and toasted them for this joyous and unforgettable moment! Now we have a beautiful granddaughter and we often look for inexpensive flights to New York to visit her. We love spending time with our granddaughter (and of course her parents).

6. Be there for their good times and trying times. Moving through life is like moving through a mountain range of peaks and valleys. Some life experiences seem like climbing the toughest mountain - in the dark without a trail map (guidance), ropes (support) or headlamp (vision). You must have the commitment and tenacity to overcome the challenges presented to you. Life is not a bowl of cherries. You will be presented with tears, smiles, falls, triumphs, and pain without warning. At times, what feels like a ton of bricks will fall on your head and shoulders. You will experience good days and challenging times. I guarantee that we all can overcome any challenge and reach the place we call peace. Time can be one factor; it can help heal the sorrows and pains. Be there for family no matter what!

Healthy Friends

"True friends are those who lift you up and put a smile on your face!"

-Hae Bolduc-

1. Good friends are true friends; keep them. True friends are there for you all the time and especially when you are going through life's ups and downs. I was going through a very dark time after I lost my first husband. One morning I woke up hearing something hitting the window. When I went outside to see what was happening, I found my dear friend cleaning all the windows in my house. He said he wanted me to see the light through every square inch of every window. He is indeed a true friend, whom I will forever cherish.

2. Drop all your Facebook "friends." Don't get distracted by the activities of others; it is background noise. You can't even tell when a Facebook friend is having a bad day and you could care less about their minute-by-minute activities. Few Facebook friends will show up at your funeral; most Facebook "friends" are not true friends. They are only a distraction in your life.

3. Keep in contact with your friends regularly by email or text. Better yet, connect with them by phone or in person over tea and hear their voice. When you are traveling, make an effort

to connect with friends. Not only will they appreciate your visit, you may even have a place to stay.

4. Send your friends birthday wishes; celebrate their kids' successes and their family events.

5. Good friends know you very well; they just have to look into your eyes to sense a glimpse of your mood and what is happening in your life. A true friend is one you can let peer into your open closet.

6. Good friends are eager to accommodate your last minute changes.

Healthy Neighbor

We live in a very peaceful location with many wonderful neighbors who shovel the snow on our sidewalk and pick up our mail while we travel. Having wonderful neighbors gives us peace of mind. We are happy to go outside and converse with neighborhood friends. No matter how often you come and go, you will run into your neighbors on a regular basis. And when you do, you should be eager to say "hi," and ask about their kids and families. Having wonderful neighbors is a blessing. When my husband got hurt during a mountain biking accident, he could not easily move, and at times had pain from his fractured pubic ramus. Our next door neighbor stopped by every morning with a cup of coffee in his hand and a smile on his face. He would ask if I needed anything, like help with grocery shopping or help with household chores. We also have a neighbor who picks up our mail when we travel for extended periods. He will even sort out and toss the junk mail, water the garden when needed, and shovel the snow on the sidewalk on snowy days. Love your neighbors like yourself.

1. Have neighborhood gatherings twice a year – around the December holidays and around the 4th of July holiday; get to know your neighbors.
2. Watch out for each other and offer to help while they are on vacation or out of town.
3. Share and exchange your perennial flowers and herbs to make the neighborhood a beautiful flower-filled environment.
4. Help your neighbors when they need a hand.
5. Be conscientious and courteous with noise and the appearance of your house and yard.
6. Have your neighbors over for a casual dinner, lunch or social gathering.

Healthy Community

Look at the resources and activities available in your community and volunteer to give back; I have written most of this book in the Colorado Springs public library 21C where I can hide and be by myself. I find that thoughts come out of nowhere when I am in this setting!

1. Local libraries are full of resources; make sure to take advantage of the available resources and periodically volunteer.
2. Look to the senior center and YMCA for volunteer opportunities and to exchange information, ideas, and teach classes.
3. The Small Business Development Center has many free resources.
4. Volunteer to work with kids at schools. Working with young children helps keep you young and vibrant.
5. Join local clubs to engage in organized activities where you can meet people and learn about local events. Join a Toastmasters club, a running club, a hiking club, a biking club, a dancing club, and/or a book club.

6. Volunteer to help at the soup kitchen, the library, or the nursing home to help those in need – Craig and I served a variety of functions when we volunteered at the Seeds Community Cafe; we were server, inventory clerk, salad preparation chef, and host! It is immediate gratification when you help others in need.

THIRTY DAY CHALLENGE

Date:

I would like to improve my relationship with:

1.
2.
3.

What are the challenges I am facing with the relationships I have stated above?

1.
2.
3.

Goals which I will set and work toward to improve my relationships:

1.
2.
3.

Chapter 2

Dream Job

. . . .

"We all have dreams. But in order
to make dreams come into reality, it
takes an awful lot of determination,
dedication, self-discipline and effort."

-Jesse Owens Olympic Gold-Medalist Runner-

~busy at work~

For five days a week, most of us spend more than 50% of our wakening hours, 8 a.m. to 5 p.m., at work. Of course, being able to pay the bills, eat, sleep in a warm comfortable bed, send the kids to school, and pay for the kids' extracurricular activities makes earning money worthwhile. But don't be a prisoner of your job! If you have a job you are passionate about, you are very good at, and one which will financially support you, then you have hit the gold mine. I worked in the technical field for over 30 years. I thought I would never work in any other area. I loved technology and the people I worked with, including my bosses and the superb team members. But at the end of day, I found I was not contributing enough and was not fully satisfied. I needed something more satisfying than just going to work for a company. So, late in my 50s I decided to do something I had been wanting to do, spend more time with my family, especially my mom, my sisters and their respective husbands and kids. Then I found my passion to write books and help inspire others to become healthy in mind, body and spirit.

1. Working in an area you are passionate about, can grow in, and can contribute to a company or society at large is the key to career success.

2. Meaningful work means doing something about which you care. Quit your job if you hate when Monday morning rolls around. I went to college thinking logically that if I graduated with a "wonderful" four year degree that, of course, I would make lots of money and have the ability to support my lifestyle. The logic is good, and then some of us may end up with a job which makes us unhappy. The job, however, pays the bills, so we become a prisoner to it. Since you are not happy with your job, you unknowingly distract yourself from your unhappiness by accumulating material possessions. This promotes further unhappiness and stress.

3. While you are working an eight-to-five job in which you are not satisfied, search for a new position that will make you thrive and help make you happy. Keep searching, try finding another job, and fail. The only way to succeed is to fail more times than you succeed.

4. Move on from your paycheck-to-paycheck job soon to dedicate your life to what you truly enjoy and gives you purpose. I have a friend who has been counting down the months to

retirement, starting at 120. Don't be a prisoner of your job, move on and find meaningful work! A couple I know recently retired and sold everything, including a home of 30 years which included a one acre lot with 35 trees. This home and "yard" required constant care and attention. They decided to leave it all behind, rent a condo, and become carefree. They moved on from the yard work and home maintenance to focus on their health and travel. What a way for them to start a new phase of life - by simply enjoying what they love the most, working on their health, hobbies, hiking, traveling, and going new places.

5. No one is born with a passion. You cultivate passion. You know it is passion when you fail and are still excited about it. Passion is when you start the day early in the morning and in what seems like no time, it is midnight and the time has just disappeared into thin air. Find your passion!

6. Have you pushed hard on the gas pedal while the car is in park?; the car only smokes and makes lots of noise. Instead, put the car in drive and keep driving toward your personal destination.

THIRTY DAY CHALLENGE

Date:

Discovering My Dream Job
Inventory of what I love:

1.
2.
3.

Inventory of what I am good at and better than anyone else:

1.
2.
3.

Discovering my economic engine (combining and turning what I love and what I am good at into my economic engine):

1.
2.
3.

Chapter 3

Financial Freedom

· ·

"Being debt free is the new American dream" –
Ryan Nicodemus - the minimalists [1]

~freedom~

You will never feel so alive and free as when you have financial freedom. You will feel like you own the world, and your worries and stress will diminish tremendously. You can reach the state of financial freedom with very little effort. My first husband and I had several properties. He was a genius on practical things. He could figure out how to fix anything that was broken and needing repair. So, it was a good match for him to manage properties and rent them out. One day, he passed away suddenly with a heart attack and I was left with all the properties; I didn't even know the location of the light switches. I was left with the tremendous burden of maintaining and renting out the properties.

Finally I decided to sell the properties, one by one. Unloading the properties was a huge weight off my shoulders. You think that by "owning" and renting properties you will get rich quickly, but it is not for everyone. If you are a Mr. Fix-it, then it might work for you, but there is no such thing as becoming quickly rich by renting out a few properties. Just like any other endeavor, if you tenaciously work at it, you will make a living.

1. Eliminate all debt except for your home mortgage. Less than 25% of your take home

pay should go toward your dwelling. If you are committed to living in the same area for at least seven years, consider buying a home, otherwise rent. The advantages of renting are as follows:

    a. No home maintenance

    b. Living simply

    c. Easy to relocate

2. Live within your means. Do not compete with your neighbors or friends for material possessions. Do not be material possessions rich because you just got a promotion and raise. Buying material items may give you temporary satisfaction, but soon you will be looking for your next acquisition.

3. Spend less than you bring in. Living paycheck to paycheck is not living; it just makes you a slave of money and your job. You should never put yourself in the position of worrying about where your next meal will come from or where you will lie down for a warm rest each night, regardless of your stage in life.

4. Save at least 25% of your paycheck for a "rainy day" and retirement. A rainy day is an unexpected, non-optional financial storm. Whenever you make extra money, put it way.

The difference between the rich and the poor is that the rich will think about how they can invest extra money and the poor will come up with ways to spend extra money. You do not have to be in debt.

5. Never have a car payment. A car should be a means of transportation from point A to point B. Paying a high price for a car is a waste of money. If you can not pay cash for a car, you should find other safe and economical means of transportation. No one will respect you because you are driving around an expensive, fancy vehicle with high monthly payments. It will only drag you down.

6. Use only one credit card with a minimum available credit and one which gives you the most benefits with a low or nonexistent annual fee. When you spend on credit, pay off the balance before the due date to avoid high interest rates. Better yet, set up autopay for the credit card to avoid late payment fees.

THIRTY DAY CHALLENGE

Date:

Step 1: Record your earnings and spending for 30 days - your salary income, all other income, and everything from a cup of coffee, train ride, entertainment, fixed monthly bills, grocery shopping, etc.

Step 2: Review the information in step 1 to determine where you may eliminate waste.

Step 3: Plan out long term goals:

> Buying a house
> Buying a car
> Retirement Travel
> Debt free

Step 4: Calculate how much and for how long you must save and refine your spending in order to meet Step 3. A retirement calculator found through google may help you with this calculation.

Chapter 4

Healthy Body for Life

. . . .

"Health is wealth" – Hae's mom

~keep moving - health for life ~

You are in charge of your health. Become the CEO of your body, thanking your body for all it does for you 24x7x365 days – non-stop. You are unique and your body is the only one you have. You must listen to it and take good care of it every day.

1. Be good every day to your body: Drink water and consume (eat) only foods that are good for your body. Mainly eat plant-based whole foods. Restrict or eliminate processed foods and cut out eggs, dairy, and meat (review the independent evidence based research extolling the only healthy diet - plant-based whole food - in Dr. Michael Greger's book, "How Not to Die.") Exercise: Run, walk, and do strength training to keep your body fit. I run four or more days a week and do strength training three days a week. My mom is 96 years old and is very healthy both mentally and physically. She still remembers what I did when I was two years old. She is very active and walks to the local community center to exercise and socialize. She mainly eats locally grown vegetables and a small amount of locally caught fish.

2. Declutter your living environment and be free of excess material possessions to destress your mind. Eliminate toxic hygiene, cleaning, and other household products (visit ewg.org to research the toxicity of common household products). Craig and I, not too long ago, each began our second marriage. When we merged

into one, we found that we had many duplicate items.

We sorted them out starting with kitchen utensils, bedroom sets, furniture, and dish sets. We only kept one set of each and only what we needed. We donated the extra items to neighborhood college kids who were just starting out in their own home and we donated items to Goodwill. We donated books to the library. By donating, not only will you be contributing to society, but the donated items will be utilized rather than collecting dust. This can give you a sense of pride.

3. Exercise your Mind: Declutter your mind by feeding it only positive thoughts. Move on from negative memories and worries about upcoming events with unknown outcomes. The only thing you need to focus on is now; everything else has either gone by or is yet to come. The best way I find to declutter my mind is through meditation, running, and hiking. When I am meditating, my mine is still, calm, and with no worries about events to come. Problems do pop up, and with time, so do potential solutions – either good or bad; as soon as you find solutions,

implement them. It's OK even if the solution fails; at least you tried to solve the problem and can move on to the next possible solution.

4. Exercise your brain: learn new languages, hobbies, and skills. My husband and I study Spanish at the local library in a free weekly class. It not only helps keep our mind sharp, but brings life to the lighter side through the social aspect. We also take salsa dance classes once per week; it is very challenging to train our brain with new body moves. It also helps keep our minds sharp. At a minimum, start reading one book per month; books lead me along a better path in life.

5. Refrain from alcohol, drugs, smoking, and obsessive eating. You do not have to be intoxicated to have a good time. Alcohol will only harm you mentally and physically.

6. Turn down the background noise by turning off the TV, the news, the commercials, the advertisements, and the gossip. This noise will not only waste your valuable time, but drain your positive energy.

THIRTY DAY CHALLENGE

Date:

I would like to improve my health in following areas:

1.
2.
3.

What are the challenges I am facing with my health in above areas?

1.
2.
3.

Goals I will set and work toward to improve my health:

1.
2.
3.

Chapter 5

Healthy Environment

. . . .

*"Organize your space and have freedom
in your life" -Hae Bolduc-*

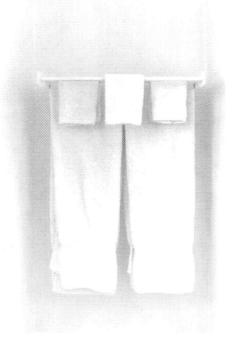

~peaceful space~

1. Declutter your living space by leaving only the items that are important to you and make your heart sing [2]. Either sell or donate everything else. Ask yourself, "What am I willing to let go of?" A few years ago, we had a very close call with an urban fire and the possibility of losing all household possessions. A forest fire with assistance from a very strong wind burned through the neighborhood and was halted by the firefighters only four blocks from our home. We were forced to evacuate. The first thought that came to our minds was, "What should we take with us from home?" It became clear that we just needed to take our computer, which contained all our financial documents, photos, scans, and our work. That's all we really needed if we were to start over. Have you ever looked into or taken a ride in your friend's, colleague's, or acquaintance's car? I have, and by looking at the environment in that person's car, I could predict the appearance of their home living space and their emotional state. I have a friend with whom I occasionally rode. Before I could enter her car, I had to move stuff off of the front passenger seat and when I glanced into the back

seat of the car, it was full of grocery bags, extra clothes, left over bagels from an undetermined distant past, water bottles, drinking cups, and coffee cups. Her home was cluttered in a similar fashion. If you have a messy car, office or home, your mind is also cluttered with messy thoughts. In order to be free, you must clean and declutter – make a habit of deep cleaning once per month or even weekly. It will help you think clearly!

2. Our current living space – Clean air, clean mountain water, clean street, away from the distracting commercial district, but close to work, cultural events, favorite activities, and stores where we can purchase needed items without spending lots of energy and commute time. How about money versus time? Bigger salary versus commute time. Most of us have been there at one time or another. For many years my daily commute was two hours – one hour each way on good days, five days a week, plus extra credit weekend commute time as I moved my way up the corporate ladder. I thought that the more I worked the quicker I would climb the corporate ladder. I found out

this is not always the case. I finally gave up my corporate job and decided to work from home, helping others become healthy in mind, body and spirit. In writing this book for others I find there are many career choices if you focus and do research.

3. Peaceful surroundings with greenery and trees. Have you ever been in the mountains hiking or camping and leave feeling refreshed and rejuvenated? Clean air is one key element to a healthy brain and body! If you continually inhale toxic fumes, you will feel sick when your body is not keeping up with the toxic cleanup. Find access to trails for running, biking, hiking, and walking - and then use them.

4. Chose a home convenient and close to local health promoting stores like Costco, Natural Grocers, REI, Trader Joes, farmers markets, and community supported agriculture (CSA). I live in the suburbs, but am also within six miles of these stores. We can all find excuses if we look for them, but once we remove those excuses we have many great choices within reach.

5. Find a patch of land where you can plant your own herbs and vegetables and see how nature can "wow" you. Oh, I love my organic garden, using only our own compost fertilizer – the joy I experience from the garden is surprisingly delightful. Every morning I step into the garden and pick fresh chard, kale, basil, and beets to make green smoothies and salads. The first time I picked my cherry tomatoes I experienced an aroma I had never experienced from store bought tomatoes. It's a beautiful and delicious experience that brings so much happiness to my daily life.

6. Experience culture – music, dance performances, festivals, art shows, libraries, and museums! Whenever I am in need of a quiet and peaceful place, I go to the Pikes Peak Library District 21C library. I cried, laughed and felt triumphant when I completely finished a sentence in this book! Find a place where you can rest and search your soul – local parks, quiet streams, a library, quiet mountain trails, and tea and coffee shops; find a place you can call yours, where you can totally lose yourself. I have several spots I go to when I am in a dark place. Either an

extreme trail like the Manitou Incline where I can't think of anything other than my breathing because I am out of air or the 21C library where I can bury my head, cry, listen to my favorite songs, and laugh.

THIRTY DAY CHALLENGE

Date:

Define what a healthy environment means to you:

1.
2.
3.

What are the challenges I face attaining a healthy environment as defined above?

1.
2.
3.

Goals I will set and work toward to live in a healthy environment:

1.
2.
3.

Chapter 6

Spirituality

. . . .

"Life is an echo; what you see is what you sent out." -Hae Bolduc-

~heaven on earth~

1. Gratitude – Be grateful for who you are and your uniqueness as an individual. You always have your own back, and don't have to rely on anyone else. You don't have to have anyone's approval to be a beautiful human being. We are all unique individuals! There are many ways to practice gratitude daily. First thing in the morning or before you go to bed, simply write in a journal five things for which you are grateful. Address the journal entries to a friend (you don't have to share your thoughts with your friend if you don't want to) if that helps keep you motivated. I was attending a small business development meeting and happened to sit next to a lady who actually presents gratitude workshops. She was also in class for help setting up a small business and we immediately felt connected. I attended her free workshops at the local library and realized how much for granted I had been taking things and for how much I have to be thankful. Yes, I have been through many challenges and dark times, but yet I need to look for the bright side and be grateful for what I have. I am grateful for my healthy body, my smart brain, good food, a comfortable place

to sleep, the clean air I breathe, the beautiful trails on which I run, the roaming mule deer I observe while running, and the cottontail rabbits on the trail encouraging me to run faster. Of course I could never run faster than the cottontails, and yet it is so fun to compete with creatures of nature. If we just look closely around us, we can imagine, and see many blessings.

2. Daily meditation – At a minimum, meditate daily for 30 minutes first thing in the morning and/or do it as the last activity before you go to sleep. Connect with your consciousness/ subconsciousness. There are many ways to start meditation, such as, using a mobile phone app featuring guided meditations or with a timer. You can find and join a meditation community for regular practice. The goal is to practice even when it seems your mediation is not making progress. You will truly benefit when you are challenged in life. Many first time meditators get frustrated with monkey mind, or the mental activity of many thoughts. Monkey mind is a perfectly normal part of our brain function. Meditation is a journey and not a destination,

therefore, you should accept what is, and not some top of the mountain destination. At the gratitude class I met another beautiful lady, and found out that she and her husband have been practicing meditation for many years. She offered a beginner's meditation class to Craig and me. After work, her husband and she came over and showed us simple techniques on how to breathe, and introduced us to a guided meditation app (Insight Timer), which I have been using daily ever since. That was the beginning of my journey to meditation and I am deeply touched by the meditation lady who is now my best friend. We became true friends with her and her husband, for which I am very grateful.

3. Focus on your inner GPS – Listen to and follow your heart. This is key to your happiness. Look inward for happiness and well-being. It's never the same beautiful place or some external material possession for which you yearn. Those are just temporary pleasures and satisfactions, never lasting happiness. Once I was really unhappy and didn't know what was going on. I looked at my husband and I felt angry without

any reason other than I was not happy. Later I found out my happiness has nothing to do with others, it is just my inner thoughts. It is my choice to be happy, and I learned to control my emotions. That realization immediately changed my emotions and attitude. Happiness is something you create for yourself.

4. Be brutally honest with yourself – You are only lying to yourself if you are not truly honest with yourself. We all face our fair share of life challenges. When challenging events happen it seems that the whole world is against us. Take an action to make a list of the current realities (what is) and write down your own remedies for these personal melees. Then prioritize and work hard at the remedies. Your inner GPS will guide you to the start and help you obtain the resources needed for solutions.

5. What is the meaning of "quality of life?" Ok, we are not super human beings. Being vulnerable is OK. We have many faults and make many mistakes in our lives. With many faults, what does "quality of life" really mean? We are not here to just sit around and drink cocktails with cherries on top. If you work toward your true

desires, the rewards will be much greater than what you get by having someone hand you the result.

6. Creating Heaven on Earth - Heaven is really here and now. Open up your senses and hear the sounds of the wind, smell the green grass, watch the white clouds in the blue sky, and taste the fresh mint. When I am with nature, this is it. This is exactly the heaven I envision and it is here in front of me to enjoy! Give true intention and focus to everything around you. Believe that we are all connected, all one. One's happiness and willingness to be happy for others contributes to all. With more of us being healthy in spirit, we are all in a much more peaceful place in this universe!

THIRTY DAY CHALLENGE

Date:

Define what healthy spirit means to me:

1.
2.
3.

What are the challenges I face achieving a healthy spirit as defined above?

1.
2.
3.

Goals I will set to work toward a healthy spirit:

1.
2.
3.

Summary

Put more than 50% into any worthwhile relationship. Know your true friends and give back to society. What is a dream job? Perhaps it is doing what you like without a huge monetary requirement. It is easy to find documentaries of young people doing what they enjoy, whether it is exploring, following an activity of passion, or living simply. When you travel, you may meet young people traveling and exploring. A simple life is possible without the responsibility of a mortgage, car payments, and a stressful job. Financial freedom is easier than most think. It is not what you have, but rather, what you experience. There is nothing more important than a healthy body and mind. Just image if either is failing and you will know what I mean. Have you ever been around someone whose life revolves around the medical profession, who always talks about doctor visits and medications? Keep active and treat your body as a temple, because that is what it really is. You will feel free by living in a clean, safe, and uncluttered environment. And finally, go inside yourself through meditation and journaling. Keep going until you realize that everything is connected. Giving back, to yourself and others should be a daily routine. Live simply. Life is magical!

Appendix - 30-Day Challenge

List goals and challenges in each category of your life and write down your own remedies and actions to each of the goals and challenges. An electronic worksheet works best. Then prioritize.

- Enlist a coach and implement an exercise routine – Fitbit, gym, running with friends
- Connect with a Health for Life coach, mentor, or friend, weekly (or monthly)
- Give yourself permission for "me time" even if it's only 30 minutes per day
- Meditate daily for 20-30 minutes
- Exercise at least 45-60 minutes, three times per week
- Eat green and colored vegetables, many colored fruits and berries, legumes, whole grains, and nuts/seeds everyday [3]
- Limit or eliminate processed food [3]
- Limit or eliminate meat, eggs and dairy [3]

** reassess your progress after 30 days and see how your life has transformed; alter the 30 day challenge again and again until "the good habits become your character." (Hae Bolduc)

References

[1] The minimalists - Joshua Fields Millburn and Ryan Nicodemus https://www.theminimalists.com/

[2] The Life-Changing Magic of Tidying Up: The Japanese Art of Decluttering and organizing by Marie Condo

[3] Dr. Michael Greger nutritionfacts.org

Acknowledgement

This book would not have been possible without Craig, my loving husband, his support, and his persistent encouragement. I would like to thank my parents, my children, grandchild, friends, strangers, and events I have encountered along the way, which, in sum total, constitute "My Life Journey!" I am grateful for my life journey, lessons, and wisdom I am able to share with others.

Printed in the United States
By Bookmasters